MELANIN BORN SPELLING BEE KINGS

GREGORY WAYNE WALTON II

Melanin Spelling Bee Kings *(Book #2 of the Melanin Born Kings Book Series).*

DEDICATION

This book is dedicated to my first-born child, my loving son, a Melanin Born King who has been my inspiration since his birth. Additionally, I hope to inspire all young black Kings with a Dream to be successful in the world.

INTRODUCTION

I have done the research for you, and it's important that you know, studies show when young black boys receive routine spelling lessons their word recognition skills increase. Also, learning to be a good speller will make reading easier, and fun for you! I hope this book gives you confidence when doing your schoolwork and assist you in creating lifelong learning skills that will help you reach all your educational goals.

I want you to know that becoming an awesome speller, is a big part of being a great student. By practicing your spelling skills daily, you will be prepared for success in your classroom. Also, your *teacher* will be excited to have such an intelligent student like you. I hope you enjoy learning new educational skills that will help you become a Spelling Bee King!

ALPHABET (ABC'S)

A – B – C – D – E – F – G – H – I –
J – K – L – M – N – O – P – Q – R –
S – T – U – V – W – X – Y – Z.

THE KING'S SPELLING BEE WORDS

1.) Write
2.) Birthday
3.) Smiling
4.) School
5.) Striving

6.) Beautiful
7.) Captain
8.) Successful
9.) Heroes
10.) Positive

As a great student, some words may challenge you to think harder than others, but you are capable of anything! And spelling will become one of your superpowers once you learn how to use your educational gifts. I want you to always remember that you have the ability to be a high achiever in life, and in the classroom!

A good tool to remember, is to practice writing the spelling words on paper to build a strong memory base.

BLACK BOYS ARE SMART...

We can spell: W – R – I – T – E

(WRITE)

BLACK BOYS ARE HAPPY...

We can spell: B – I – R – T – H – D – A – Y

(Birthday)

BLACK BOYS ARE HELPFUL...

We can spell: S – M – I – L – I – N – G

(Smiling)

BLACK BOYS ARE FRIENDLY...

We can spell: S – C – H – O – O – L

(School)

BLACK BOYS ARE COOL...

We can spell: S – T – R – I – V – I – N – G

(Striving)

BLACK BOYS ARE LOVING...

We can spell: B – E – A – U – T – I – F – U – L

(Beautiful)

BLACK BOYS ARE LEADERS...

We can spell: C – A – P – T – A – I – N

(Captain)

BLACK BOYS ARE CAPABLE...

We can spell: S – U – C – C – E – S – S – F – U – L

(Successful)

BLACK BOYS ARE STRONG...

We can spell: H – E – R – O – E – S

(Heroes)

BLACK BOYS ARE CREATIVE...

We can spell: P – O – S – I – T – I – V – E

(Positive)

As a young student, learning to spell vocabulary words will help you to develop a good connection between the letters and their special sounds. Additionally, this skill will really improve your reading, and writing abilities that can lead to a bright future of educational success. Always remember that you're intelligent, you are a *Melanin Born King*, and your skin color is BEAUTIFUL!

Now that you're the "Spelling Bee King" smile and be proud of your BIG achievement! I want you to get excited about the new skills you've gained and go show your friends and family how well you can spell! Don't forget, practice makes us better!